SOIL

EARLY BIRD EARTH SCIENCE

BY SALLY M WALKER

LERNER BOOKS • LONDON • NEW YORK • MINNEAPOLIS

This book was first published in the United States of America in 2007.

First published in the United Kingdom in 2008 by
Lerner Books,
Dalton House,
60 Windsor Avenue,
London SW19 2RR

Website address: www.lernerbooks.co.uk

This edition was updated and edited for UK publication by Discovery Books Ltd., Unit 3, 37 Watling Street, Leintwardine, Shropshire SY7 0LW

British Library Cataloguing in Publication Data

Walker, Sally M.
Soil. - (Early bird Earth science)
1. Soils - Juvenile literature 2. Soil formation - Juvenile literature
I. Title
631.4

ISBN-13: 978 1 58013 356 2

The photographs in this book are used with the permission of: PhotoDisc Royalty Free by Getty Images, pp 1, 1(title type), 4, 6 (background), 9, 10 (background), 24 (background), 28 (background), 32, 37, 38 (both), 40, 44–45 (background), 46–47 (background); © Yoshio Tomii/SuperStock, p 5; © Dana Richter/Visuals Unlimited, p 6; © Mark A. Schneider/Visuals Unlimited, p 7; © Royalty-Free/CORBIS, pp 8, 25; © Dr. Marli Miller/Visuals Unlimited, pp 10, 15, 23; © John R. Kreul/Independent Picture Service, p 11; © Robert & Jean Pollock/Visuals Unlimited, p 12; courtesy of Captain Budd Christman/National Oceanic and Atmospheric Administration Central Library Photo Collection, p 13; © Adam Jones/Visuals Unlimited, p 14; USDA Photo, p 16; © Dr Dennis Kunkel/Visuals Unlimited, pp 17, 30; © R F Ashley/Visuals Unlimited, p 18; © Todd Strand/Independent Picture Service, pp 19, 21 (both); US Geological Survey Photo Library, pp 20, 24; © Gilbert Twiest/Visuals Unlimited, p 22; © Dr G Prance/Visuals Unlimited, p 26; © John Sohlden/Visuals Unlimited, p 28; © Todd Strand/Independent Picture Service, with permission from Munsell/Division of GretagMacbeth, LLC, p 29; © age fotostock/SuperStock, pp 33, 41; © Wally Eberhart/Visuals Unlimited, pp 34, 35, 48; © Natalia Brand/SuperStock, p 36; © Mark Gibson/Visuals Unlimited, p 39; © Pegasus/Visuals Unlimited, p 43; © Dr. John D Cunningham/Visuals Unlimited, p 46; © Bill Banaszewski/Visuals Unlimited, p 47

Front Cover: © Royalty-Free/CORBIS
Front Cover Title Type: PhotoDisc Royalty Free by Getty Images
Back Cover: © Reuters/CORBIS
Illustrations on pp 27, 31, 42 by Laura Westlund, copyright © by Independent Picture Service.

Printed in China

CONTENTS

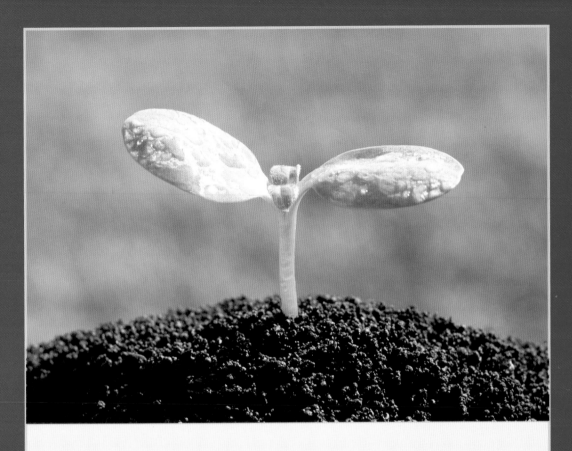

BE A WORD DETECTIVE

Can you find these words as you read about soil? Be a detective and try to work out what they mean. You can turn to the glossary on page 46 for help.

bacteria	horizon	nutrients
bedrock	humus	particles
clay	loam	sand
conserve	minerals	silt
glaciers	natural resource	textures

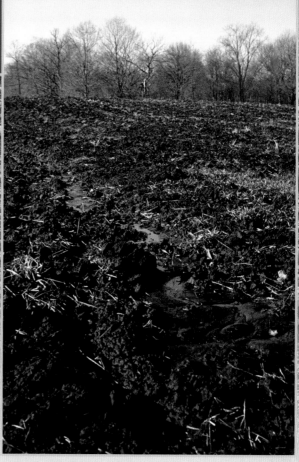

This field has good soil. A farmer will grow plants in the soil. What are some other places where soil can be found?

CHAPTER 1
WHAT IS SOIL?

Did you ever make mud pies when you were little? If you did, soil was one of the ingredients you used. You may have called it dirt instead of soil.

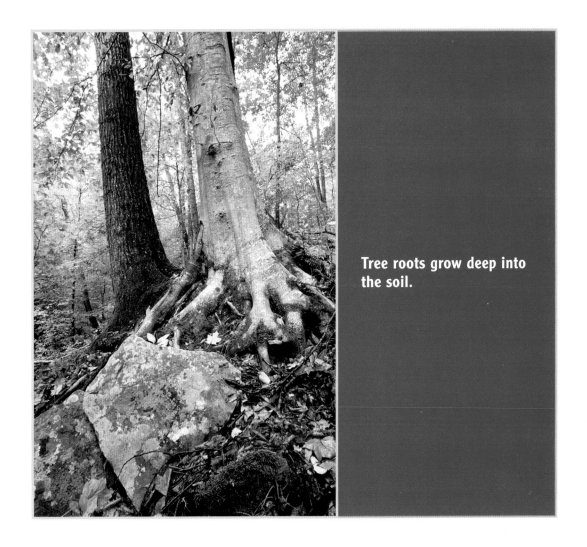

Tree roots grow deep into the soil.

Soil is in lots of places. You can find soil under the grass. It surrounds tree and flower roots. It lies beneath pavements and streets. If you could lift your house up you would probably find soil under it too!

A handful of soil contains many things. Soil has rocks in it. Plants and bits of leaves are in soil. Many creatures live in soil too.

You can be a soil detective. See what you can find in the soil near your home. You will need a spade. Ask an adult where you may dig. Use your spade to dig out several handfuls of soil. Look closely at your soil. What can you find in it?

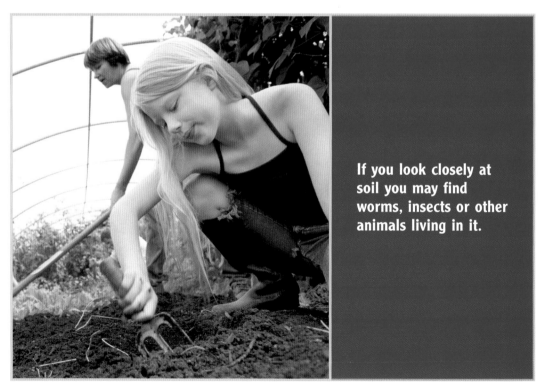

If you look closely at soil you may find worms, insects or other animals living in it.

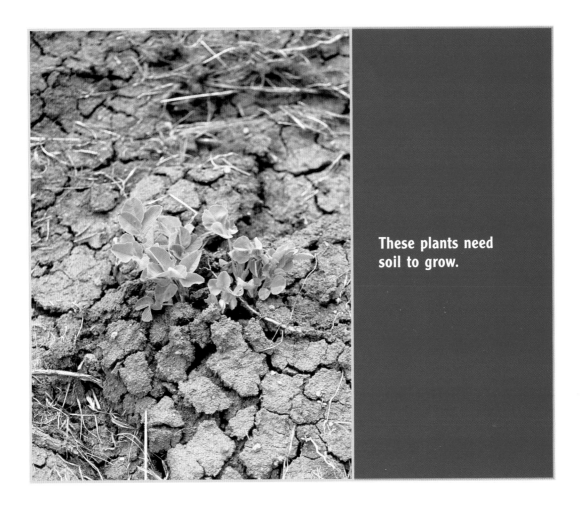

These plants need soil to grow.

Soil is a natural resource. Natural resources are materials found on Earth that help living things. They are made by nature, not people. Soil helps plants and animals grow. They cannot live without it. But where does soil come from?

Hard rocks can break into small pieces. How can water break rocks?

CHAPTER 2
HOW SOIL FORMS

Soil is made up of different kinds of materials. One of these materials is bits of rock. Rocks are broken pieces of bedrock. Bedrock is the layer of solid rock that covers the outside of the Earth.

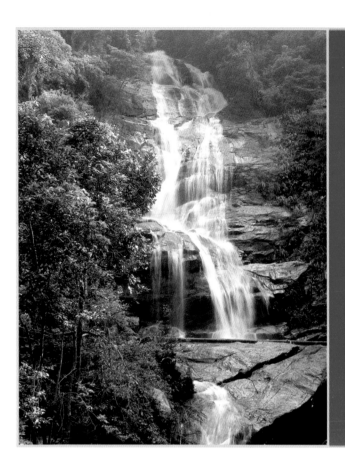

As water rushes down this hill it breaks off bits of rock.

Rocks are hard, but they can be broken into tiny bits. Tiny bits are called particles. Water, ice and wind are strong enough to break rocks.

Rushing water in rivers makes rocks roll and tumble. The rocks break into smaller pieces. Tiny particles of rock break loose.

Rainwater seeps into cracks in rocks. If it gets cold enough the water freezes. It becomes ice. Ice takes up more space than water. The ice pushes against the rock and makes the cracks bigger. Pieces of rock break off.

Ice split this huge rock in half.

This glacier is flowing downhill. As it moves it carries rocks with it.

Glaciers are giant, moving rivers of ice. Glaciers are very powerful. They slowly grind big rocks into small pieces.

Wind blows sand grains against big rocks. The sand grains scrub off particles of the rocks. Rocks are made of minerals. A mineral is a hard substance made in nature. Minerals are not alive, like plants or animals. The minerals in a rock become part of the soil when the rock breaks apart.

Grains of sand are tiny. But if the wind blows them hard enough they can break off bits of rock.

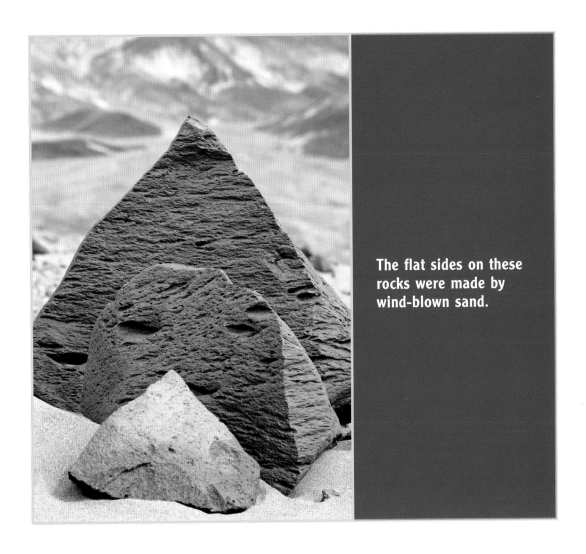

The flat sides on these rocks were made by wind-blown sand.

Minerals are an important part of soil. They add nutrients to soil. Nutrients are substances that help living things grow. Soil contains nutrients that plants and animals need to stay healthy.

Bacteria are turning these dead leaves into humus.

Humus is the second material that is in soil. Humus is dark brown or black. It is made of bits of dead plants and animals.

Humus is made by bacteria. Bacteria are tiny living things. They are so tiny that they can be seen only with a microscope. Microscopes are tools that make small things look big.

Bacteria eat dead plants and animals. They break the plants and animals into tiny pieces. The pieces become humus. Humus contains nutrients that had been inside the plants and animals. The nutrients can become part of the soil.

There are many kinds of bacteria. They live nearly everywhere on the Earth. This picture shows one kind of bacteria that lives in soil.

Air is the third material in soil. Soil is full of air spaces. Some air spaces are large. You can easily see them. You can see the tunnels that earthworms dig in soil. An earthworm's hole is filled with air. Soil also has tiny air spaces. The tiny spaces are between bits of minerals and humus. Most of these spaces are too small for you to see, but they are there.

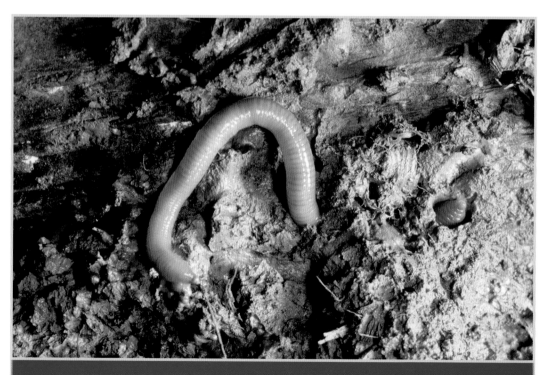

As earthworms move through the soil they make tunnels.

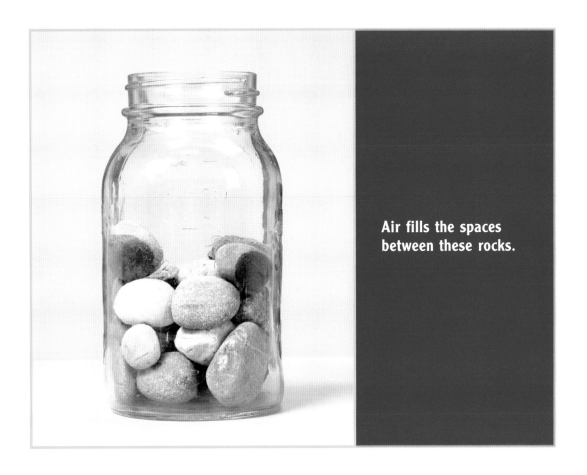

Air fills the spaces between these rocks.

Put a handful of marbles or small rocks in a jar. Can you see spaces between the marbles or rocks? Air fills these spaces. Now imagine that you can shrink the marbles or rocks. Imagine making them as tiny as the smallest particles in soil. The air spaces would still be there. They would just be much smaller.

Water is the fourth material found in soil. Water can move around in soil. It trickles through the soil's air spaces. The moving water picks up nutrients from the soil. The water carries the nutrients into the roots of plants.

Water has filled the air spaces in this soil.

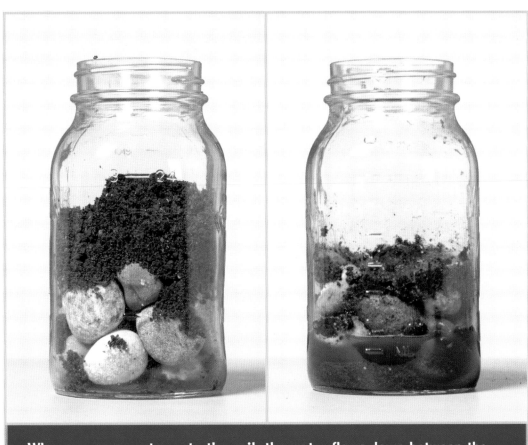

When you pour water onto the soil, the water flows down between the rocks. The water carries bits of soil with it.

Water also carries tiny particles of soil into the big air spaces. Put a handful of soil on top of the marbles or rocks in your jar. Pour in a small glass of water. Where does the water go? What happens to the particles of soil?

Soil forms on flat land. It forms alongside rivers. It forms on forest floors and on low hills. Soil forms as humus and rock particles begin to pile up. It can take hundreds of years for 2 centimetres of soil to form.

Deep soil has formed on this flat land.

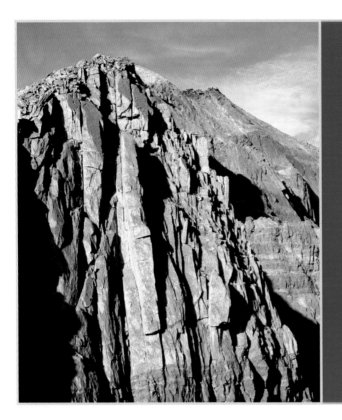

Soil can't form on the steep sides of this mountain.

Soil cannot form in some places. Soil cannot form on steep mountainsides. That's because soil-making materials slide down the mountain. Soil cannot form in very windy places or places where water flows quickly. In these places soil-making materials can't pile up. They do not have enough time to become soil.

We usually see only the top of the soil. What is this soil mostly made of?

CHAPTER 3

LAYERS OF SOIL

If you dig deep down into the ground you may notice different colours of soil. These are different layers of soil. A layer is a single thickness of soil. A blanket lying on your bed is a layer. A cake may have several layers. Soil has layers too.

This soil is made mostly of humus. It is full of nutrients that growing plants need.

A soil layer is called a horizon. The horizon that is closest to the surface is called the A horizon. This layer is made mostly of humus. The A horizon has many nutrients. It helps plants grow.

Under the A horizon is the B horizon. The B horizon has less humus. It has more sand and small rocks.

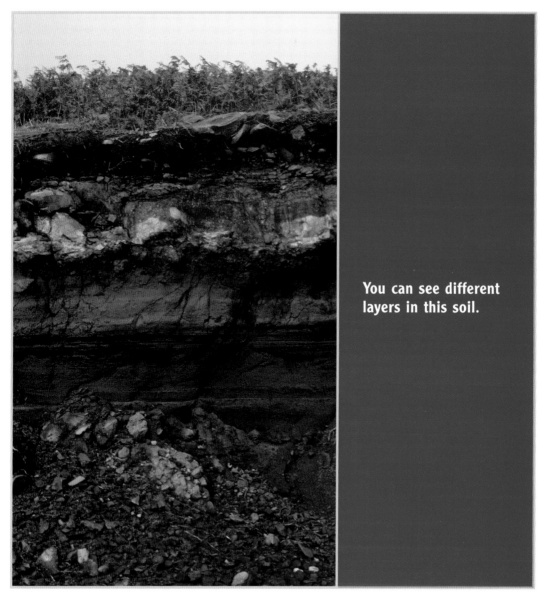

You can see different layers in this soil.

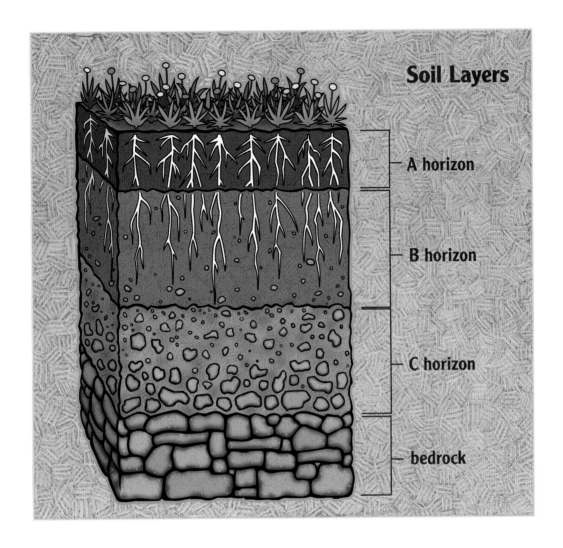

- A horizon
- B horizon
- C horizon
- bedrock

The C horizon is the lowest soil layer. It is just above the bedrock. The soil in the C horizon has lots of big, chunky rocks in it. The A and B horizons cover the C horizon. They protect the C horizon from water, ice and wind.

Most soils are brownish, but some are other colours, such as red. What gives soil its colour?

CHAPTER 4

WHAT SOIL LOOKS LIKE

Soil can be made of many different kinds of minerals. Different minerals can be different colours. The minerals and humus in soil help give the soil its colour. Many soils are a shade of brown, but some are yellow. Some are even a bright orangey red.

This chart shows some of the colours soil can be.

Soil also has different textures. Texture is how rough or smooth something is. The texture of soil depends on the size of the soil's particles.

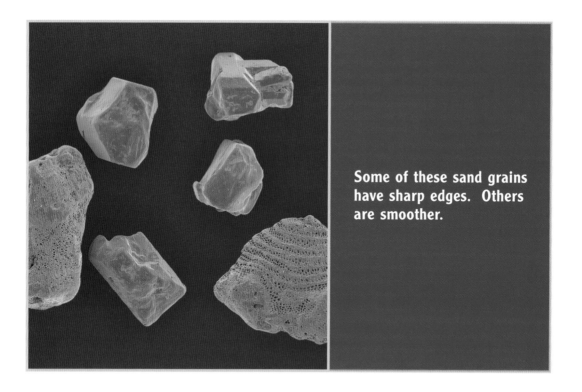

Some of these sand grains have sharp edges. Others are smoother.

The largest mineral particles in soil are called sand. You can see the mineral particles in sandy soil. Sand particles feel rough when you rub them between your fingers. Some sand particles have sharp, jagged edges. Others are more rounded.

Another kind of particle in soil is called silt. Silt particles are much smaller than sand particles. It's hard to see silt particles. If you rub silt between your fingers it feels smooth. Silt-sized particles are shaped like sand particles.

Clay particles are the smallest particles in soil. They are too small to see without a microscope. Clay particles are flat.

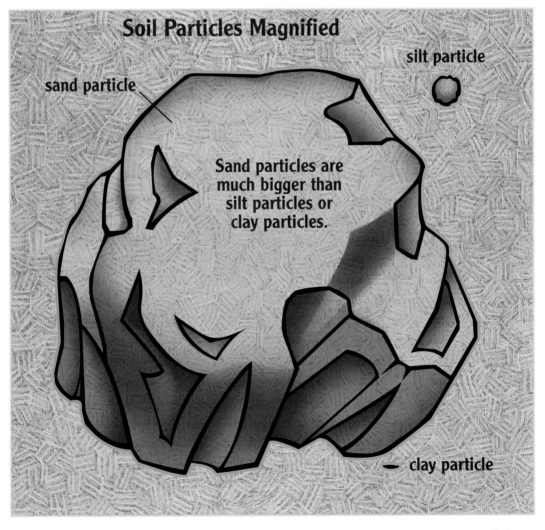

Soil Particles Magnified

silt particle

sand particle

Sand particles are much bigger than silt particles or clay particles.

clay particle

Water drains quickly through sand. That's why you won't see puddles in wet sand at the beach.

Sand particles have big air spaces between them. Water drains quickly through the spaces so puddles rarely form in sandy soil. Silt particles have smaller spaces between them. Water takes longer to drain through small spaces. Flat clay particles get squeezed together. The spaces between clay particles are tiny. Water has a hard time trickling through tiny air spaces. Clay particles also soak up water. So it takes a long time for water to drain through soil that has a lot of clay.

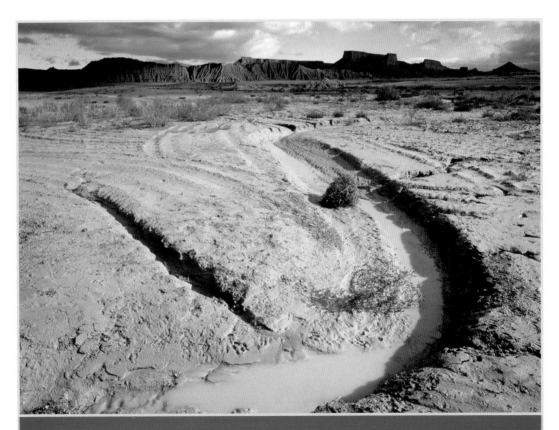

Water drains slowly through clay particles. When it rains, puddles often form in soil that has many clay particles.

Soil that has mostly sand-sized particles is called sandy loam. Water drains quickly through sandy loam. Soil with mostly clay-sized particles is called

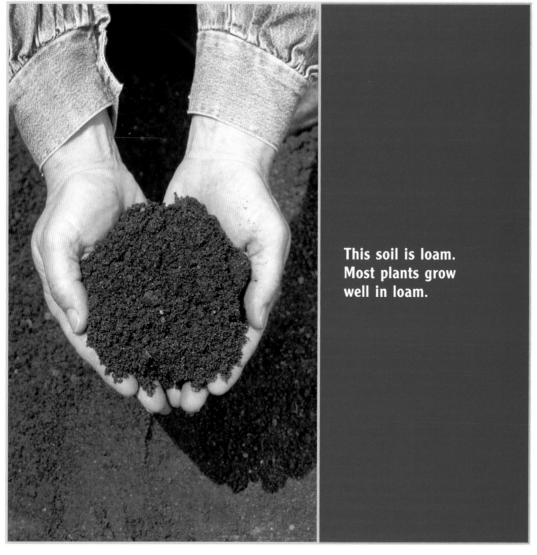

This soil is loam. Most plants grow well in loam.

This picture shows sandy soil (left), **loam** (middle), **and clay soil** (right).

clay loam. Water drains slowly through clay loam. Rain often forms puddles in clay loam.

What kind of texture does your soil have? Rub the soil between your fingers. Does it feel rough, smooth or in between?

Put some soil in your palm. Add a small
amount of water to your soil. Add only enough
to make the soil moist. If it seems too wet add

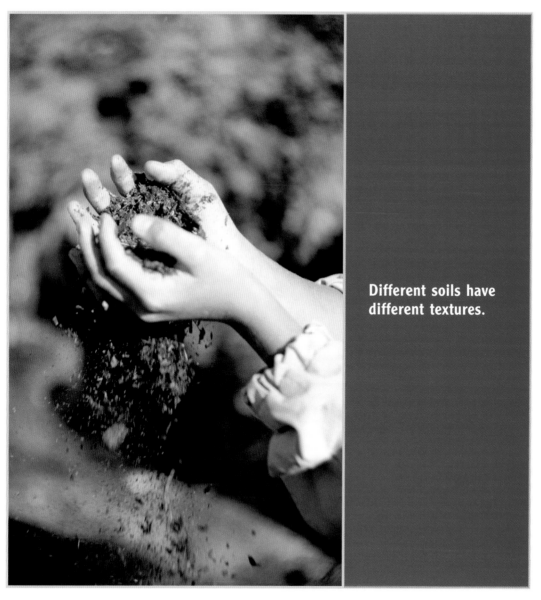

Different soils have
different textures.

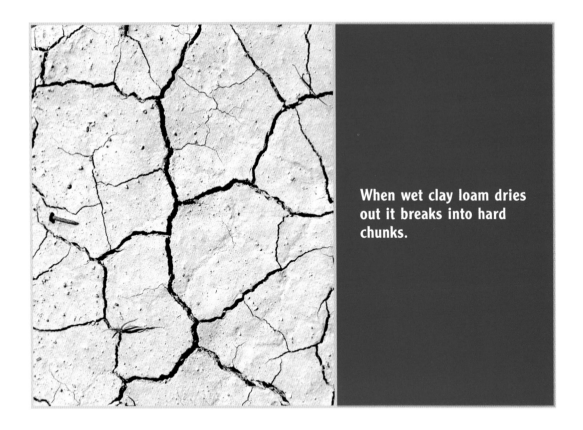

When wet clay loam dries out it breaks into hard chunks.

a little more soil. Mix the soil and water together with your fingers. See if you can mould the soil into a flat circle. If you can, your soil has a lot of clay. If the circle crumbles, the soil contains more sand and silt than clay.

We need soil so trees and other plants can grow. What happens when people spray chemicals outside?

CHAPTER 5

TAKING CARE OF SOIL

Soil is a very important natural resource. It takes a long time for soil to form. So we must take good care of the Earth's soil.

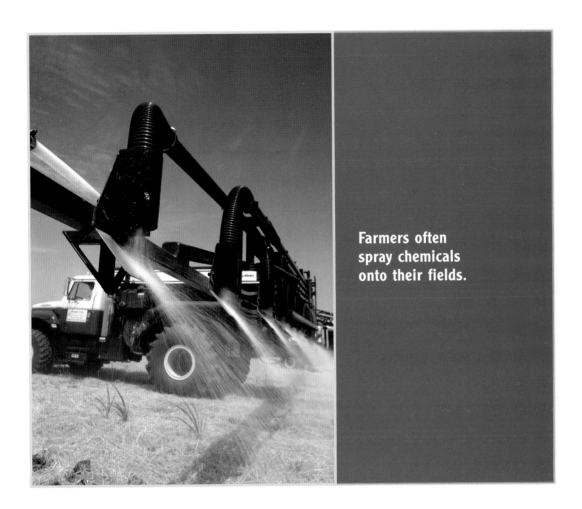

Farmers often spray chemicals onto their fields.

People often use chemicals to kill harmful bugs or weeds. Some of these chemicals may stay in the soil. The chemicals can hurt animals, people and other plants. So people must be careful not to use too much of these chemicals.

This place was once a forest. People cut down most of the trees. Rain has washed away a lot of the soil.

Tree roots help hold soil in place. Cutting down too many trees leaves the soil unprotected, then water and wind can sweep the soil away.

Farmers plant crops in soil. A crop is a kind of plant, such as potatoes or wheat. A farmer can damage soil by planting the same crop in the same field year after year. The crop uses up the soil's nutrients. After a while plants can no longer grow in that field. Wise farmers conserve soil. Conserving soil means using it wisely. Growing different crops every few years keeps a field's soil healthy. Then the field can be used for a longer time.

Different kinds of crops are growing on this farm.

rain

flowing water

furrow

soil

A farmer's plough digs furrows in the ground for planting seeds. If the furrows go from the top to the bottom of a hill, rain can run down the hill. The rain carries soil with it.

rain

furrow

If the furrows go along the side of the hill, they catch the rain. The furrows stop the rain carrying soil down the hill.

Farmers also conserve soil by ploughing their fields the right way. If the farmer ploughs furrows straight down a hill rain can easily wash soil away. Instead the farmer can make furrows that circle around the hill. Then the furrows make ridges of soil. The ridges stop the rain washing the soil away.

The next time you go outside look at the soil around you. Notice its colour. See what kinds of plants are growing in it. Feel its texture.

Watch how people take care of the soil. Try to think of ways that you can care for the soil around your house. Plants, animals and people will always need healthy soil!

Taking care of the soil is important.

ON SHARING A BOOK

When you share a book with a child, you show that reading is important. To get the most out of the experience, read in a comfortable, quiet place. Turn off the television and limit other distractions, such as telephone calls. Be prepared to start slowly. Take turns reading parts of this book. Stop occasionally and discuss what you're reading. Talk about the photographs. If the child begins to lose interest, stop reading. When you pick up the book again, re-read the parts you have already read.

BE A VOCABULARY DETECTIVE

The word list on page 5 contains words that are important in understanding the topic of this book. Be word detectives and search for the words as you read the book together. Talk about what the words mean and how they are used in the sentence. Do any of these words have more than one meaning? You will find the words defined in a glossary on page 46.

WHAT ABOUT QUESTIONS?

Use questions to make sure the child understands the information in this book. Here are some suggestions:

> What did this paragraph tell us? What does this picture show? What are the four materials found in soil? How does water break rocks into smaller pieces? What are some places where soil can't form? What are layers of soil called? What are the three sizes of mineral particles in soil? What is your favourite part of the book? Why?

If the child has questions, don't hesitate to respond with questions of your own, such as What do *you* think? Why? What is it that you don't know? If the child can't remember certain facts, turn to the index.

INTRODUCING THE INDEX

The index helps readers find information without searching through the whole book. Turn to the index on page 48. Choose an entry such as *humus* and ask the child to find out what humus is made of. Repeat with as many entries as you like. Ask the child to point out the differences between an index and a glossary. (The index helps readers find information, while the glossary tells readers what words mean.)

LEARN MORE ABOUT
SOIL

BOOKS

Fleming, Sarah. *How to Make Soil* (Treetops Non-Fiction) Oxford University Press, 2005.

Gannett, Barbara. *It's All in the Soil* (Four Corners) Longman, 2004.

Oxlade, Chris. *Soil* (Materials, Materials, Materials) Heinemann Library, 2002.

WEBSITES

The Dirt on Soil
http://school.discovery.com/schooladventures/soil/
Learn about the layers of soil and some of the creatures that live there, then go on an underground adventure.

Kids and Conservation
http://www.clarkswcd.org/Kids/KidsHome.htm
Learn how people can conserve soil, water and wildlife.

Mineral Matters
http://www.sdnhm.org/kids/minerals/
This website has information about minerals, instructions for growing your own crystals, puzzles and more.

Soil Layers
http://www.enchantedlearning.com/geology/soil/
This web page has information about all of the soil's layers.

Natural History Museum
http://www.nhm.ac.uk
This site for the Natural History Museum in London has a large amount of information on rocks, minerals and the Earth's processes. It also has a great section especially for children.

GLOSSARY

bacteria: tiny living things that can be seen only with a microscope

bedrock: the layer of solid rock that covers the outside of the Earth

clay: the smallest mineral particles in soil

conserve: to stop something being lost or wasted

glaciers: giant, moving rivers of ice. Glaciers form in places that are cold all year round.

horizon: a layer of soil

humus: a dark brown or black substance that is a part of soil. Humus is made of bits of dead plants and animals.

loam: soil that has equal amounts of sand, silt and clay particles. Loam is very good for growing plants.

minerals: hard substances that are made in nature. Minerals are not alive, like plants or animals.

natural resource: a material found on Earth that helps living things. It is made by nature, not people.

nutrients: substances that help living things grow

particles: tiny bits

sand: the largest mineral particles in soil

silt: medium-sized mineral particles in soil. Silt particles are smaller than sand particles, but larger than clay particles.

textures: the roughness or smoothness of different objects

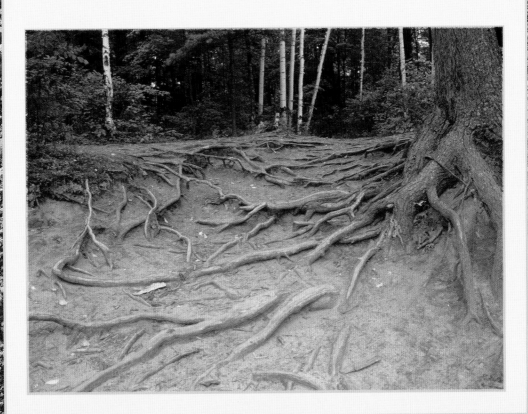

INDEX

Pages listed in **bold** type refer to photographs.